POSTAGE
STAMPS AS
PROPAGANDA

By Carlos Stoetzer

Postage Stamps
As Propaganda

CARLOS STOETZER

Public Affairs Press, Washington, D. C.

CONTENTS

CONSTERNATION ran high when officials of West Berlin recently discovered that the envelopes of letters arriving from the Soviet sector of that city were being imprinted with totalitarian propaganda. This sort of thing could hardly be countenanced by the democratic postal authorities, but what were they to do? Since they could not make the Communists discontinue their propaganda, they stamped a highly effective retort on those envelopes from the Communist East which bore the slogan "Learn from the Soviet People and the Great Stalin how to build socialism." Directly beneath these words the West Berlin post office put its own stamp: "And what has resulted from it."

The postage stamp and the postal cancellation constitute a comparatively new propaganda medium of which people are little aware. Today this medium is being used quite intensively.

However, since propaganda on postage stamps is of a more subdued and discreet nature than that exhibited by other media, it has been given surprisingly little attention. Yet the fact that the postage stamp is widely circulated and that it does not have an obvious message enhances its peculiar effectiveness.

The stamp itself is ideal propaganda. It goes from hand to hand and town to town; it reaches the farthest corners and provinces of a country and even the farthest countries of the world. It is a symbol of the nation from which the stamp is mailed, a vivid expression of that country's culture and civilization and of its ideas and ideals. By the use of symbols, slogans, pictures, even loaded words, it conveys its message far and wide.

The postage stamp as such has had a rather short existence. Prior to 1840 there was none. A person desiring to send a letter took it to the post office where it was weighed, marked with the amount to be paid, and sent on, the postage being paid by the addressee upon receipt of the letter.

A revolutionary change came in 1840, when Sir Rowland Hill founded his penny postage system in England. For a long time thereafter the purpose of the postage stamp remained primarily and uniquely a postal one. The stamp simply represented the fee pay-

1

able for the transportation and delivery of a letter or parcel. The state, which usually administered the postal services—except in Central Europe where the private enterprise of the famous Thurn and Taxis Mail Administration fulfilled the task until 1866—was interested only in collecting payment for the postal services it rendered to the individual. In those days the cancellation was only a mark to obliterate and cancel the stamp and show the place and time of dispatch.

Indeed, the epoch in philately from 1840 until World War I and shortly thereafter may be called the classical—i.e., non-propagandistic period. The designs represented on stamps in this era were, like those on coins, of an obvious nature and did not serve any secondary purpose. In monarchies, the head of the dynasty or the coat of arms was usually shown; in republics, either the coat of arms, some symbolic allegory or a representation of the founding fathers was depicted. To give some examples, England and her colonies always represented the head of the monarch (Queen Victoria, King Edward VII, King George V), as did Spain (Queen Isabella II, King Amadeo, King Alfonso XII, King Alfonso XIII) and Belgium (King Leopold I, King Leopold II, King Albert I). The coat of arms was depicted in other countries such as Argentina, Germany, Turkey, Russia, Austria, Haiti and the Dominican Republic. Symbolic allegories were pictured on French stamps (la République, Cérès), German stamps (Germania), Swiss stamps (Helvetia) and Greek stamps (Hermes). The founding fathers were generally represented on stamps of the United States as well as on stamps of the other American republics. Some countries —Brazil and Bavaria, for example—showed only numbers. By and large, however, the stamp remained a purely functional piece of paper.

Until World War I there were relatively few stamp collectors, but with the increasingly widespread interest in philately the postage stamp evolved from its original purely utilitarian role. From a tiny, inconsequential piece of paper, it grew larger and larger, depicting more or less every aspect of national and international life. It became in considerable degree a miniature advertising poster.

An important factor in the evolution of the postage stamp was the gradual realization by many governments of the immense source of income which stamps could provide. Hence, most stamps, particularly in the 1920's and afterwards, lost their purely postal character in favor of other ends. Some countries began to give philatelic issues their special attention in order to derive a sizable part of the national income from the sale of stamps. Significantly enough, countries such

2

as Monaco, San Marino, Liechtenstein and Liberia now receive a large proportion of their revenue from the frequent issuance and sale of new sets of stamps to collectors all over the world. To enhance sales, they print stamps which are really artistic works, ranking among the very finest engravings.

Once the various countries recognized postage stamps as a substantial source of income, they began to sense how, through philately, they could publicize and promote certain tourist, cultural, economic, historical and political aims. Thus the postage stamp gradually came to fulfill three purposes: (a) delivering mail; (b) increasing the national income; and (c) spreading propaganda. Today virtually every state is engaged in the battle of world philately in two ways—conquering new markets for stamps, and using them as a propaganda vehicle. The growing importance of the propaganda aspect of mail has been further demonstrated by those countries which cover envelopes with special markings, posters, labels and cancellations.

A sizable proportion of the population of every country is now stamp conscious. In the United States alone there are more than ten million collectors. The immensity of the volume of mail in circulation is indicated by the fact that New York City alone distributes over 19,000,000 letters, 125,000 pieces of registered mail and 319,000 pounds of newspapers and publications daily.

It is not only the philatelist and the dealer who are stamp conscious. The layman is most certainly attracted by an envelope if it has a beautifully designed, artistic stamp or an unusual marking, especially if it comes from abroad. At that moment propaganda starts its work.

Philatelic propaganda reaches not only the recipient of the letter, but also everyone who has handled the letter, starting with the individual who mails it. The envelope passes through many hands in the different postal offices, and goes through many cities, and often through many countries before reaching its final destination.

Of importance is the ever growing number of postage stamp exhibitions, national as well as international. At these meetings a great deal of propaganda is carried out, intentionally and unintentionally.

With the ever increasing interrelationship of national economies, the raising of the educational level in many parts of the world, the advances of technology, the spread of democracy, the world in a sense has become much smaller than it used to be, and postal services have come to play an increasingly important and extensive role.

3

As the passion to collect stamps has developed throughout the world and as peoples have progressed in education and culture, each country has made vigorous efforts through stamps to further national and even nationalistic goals. Today governments are unabashedly using postage stamps to promote domestic products, vacation resorts, cultural achievements, and even political ideologies.

Tourist Propaganda

As the tourist business has gained ground everywhere in recent years, postal authorities have more and more sought to advertise the beautiful resorts, picturesque landscapes, and attractive cities of their countries to induce visitors to flock in and spend their dollars, pounds, and francs.

Stamps depicting the beauties of a country have a manifold propaganda aim. They advertise abroad as well as at home famous places so that tourists, adventure-lovers and globetrotters may be lured to spend their next vacation in one of the advertised spas or resorts. For the native they constitute propaganda aimed at increasing his national pride. Even people who cannot afford to travel are influenced; beautiful scenery on a stamp tends to favorably affect their attitude towards a foreign country. If the stamps are well-designed, the sponsoring state can usually count on receiving some additional source of income (unless the issue has too obviously been used for non-postal purposes or is of a speculative nature) from collectors attracted by aesthetic engravings.

Among the first to depict natural beauties on stamps was New Zealand in 1898. Austro-Hungarian postal authorities in Bosnia-Herzegovina followed suit in 1906, when they released a famous set of landscapes. At the beginning, countries which used tourist propaganda showed only the most important subjects, the symbols by which the country was known throughout the world. Thus, Brazil pictured the Sugarloaf Mountain; Greece, the Acropolis; Egypt, the Pyramids and the Sphinx; Switzerland, the Alps; Japan, Fujiyama; and Turkey, the Golden Horn. Later, as travel increased, some countries not only showed pictures of their less known scenic spots, but released glamorized views of places depicted somewhat monotonously on earlier stamps.

4

The more nations became tourist conscious, the more their postal authorities used stamps for travel promotion purposes.

The Netherlands released special stamps (the "Salve Hospes" issue) to promote tourism in 1932. This set was intended to lure the foreign visitor by portraying typically Dutch landscapes.

British, Dutch, French, Portuguese, Spanish and Belgian colonies rivalled the European countries in depicting their beautiful scenery in an effort to conquer the hearts of both philatelist and tourist. Travel poster stamps even began to publicize the hundreds of islands in the Pacific—Fiji, Samoa, Niue, Pitcairn, Tonga, Papua, New Caledonia and Nauru, to cite a few.

In the old days, tourists who came to a resort country could visit only the most important places, but now that air travel has largely cut the time needed for travel, previously inaccessible spots are being publicized on postage stamps. The Caribbean countries in particular have taken advantage of this factor to advertise their touristic attractions. Cuba, Jamaica, Haiti and Trinidad, among others, have issued stamps showing points of interest besides their capitals. Perhaps the greatest drive for tourist trade is the new Dominican Republic hotel issue, which depicts the leading hotels of that country to convince the potential visitor that modern accommodations await him.

The most famous set of tourist stamps issued by the United States was the National Park series of 1934, which made millions of Americans anxious to see for themselves the great parks administered by the Department of Interior. Argentina and Japan also released national park sets for essentially the same purpose.

So extensive has been the use of tourist scenes upon postage stamps as a means of publicizing scenic beauty, that the average philatelist can well feel he can see the whole world through his postage stamps.

Cultural Propaganda

It has become customary for nearly every country to use its postage stamps to advertise and diffuse its culture abroad and to show to both the world and its own people the high standards it has reached. The United States, for example, issued in 1940 various sets of famous American poets, musicians, educators, writers, artists, inventors, and scientists. Among those depicted were Washington Irving, James

Fenimore Cooper, Stephen Foster, John Philip Sousa, Horace Mann, Booker T. Washington, Henry Wadsworth Longfellow, John Greenleaf Whittier, John Audubon, Walter Reed, James Whistler, Gilbert Stuart, Alexander Graham Bell, and Samuel Morse.

France uses its stamps mostly for cultural propaganda. Early in 1923 Pasteur was represented on a regular set of stamps which remained in circulation until 1927. The poet Ronsard and the chemist Berthelot were likewise portrayed on stamps at about this time. After 1936 six or seven new stamps containing cultural propaganda were added yearly. Besides these individual cultural stamps, France has been issuing annually whole sets bearing famous Frenchmen of each century. For example, the seventeenth century set, which appeared in 1944, depicted Molière, Mansart, Pascal, Condé, Colbert and Louis XIV.

In addition to portraying famous men on their stamps to express cultural nationalism, the nations of the world also make use of heraldry, great literary works, regional costumes, exhibitions, pottery, archaeological sites and museums, flowers, and historical events. To give but a few examples, heraldry has been depicted on stamps by Belgium (1941, 1946), France (1941-1946), and Germany (1925-1929); great literary works by Austria (1926), Finland (1935), Italy (1924, 1930, 1936), Latvia (1930), Portugal (1924, 1925), and Spain (1902); regional costumes by Austria (1934, 1948), France (1938, 1939, 1943), Germany (1935), and Portugal (1941, 1947); exhibitions by Argentina (1943, 1946), and Belgium (1894, 1930, 1935, 1939); pottery by Greece (1896), and Spanish Morocco (1946); archaeological sites and museums by Guatemala (1942), Mexico (1924, 1934), Peru (1938), Syria (1924, 1930), and Tunisia (1906, 1926); flowers by Israel (1952) and Switzerland (1943, 1944, 1945, etc.); and historical events by Bulgaria (1942), Lithuania (1932), and Poland (1938).

In Italy, particularly under Mussolini, much has been done to call attention to the country's outstanding past. The famous men series of 1932 showing renowned Italians is an example of this trend. Besides such poets as Dante, Ariosto, and Tasso, the Italian stamps honored Leonardo da Vinci, Macchiavelli and other cultural figures of renown. Ancient Roman figures such as Virgil, Augustus, and Horace, were also used to emphasize that modern Italy is linked to the glories of old Rome.

Another country which has indulged heavily in cultural propaganda is Austria. Large sets of Austrian stamps depict musicians, architects, painters, military men, cities, poets, the Nibelungen saga, inventors and doctors. A stamp of special interest to Americans was that put out in 1949 to honor Gruber and Mohr, the composers of the famous Christmas carol, "Silent Night."

Wagner, Bach, Goethe, Schiller and Zeppelin in Germany; Grieg, Nansen and Ibsen in Norway; Eminescu in Rumania; Rubens, Piccard, Charlemagne and other historical personalities in Belgium; Erasmus and Rembrandt in Holland; Lope de Vega and Cervantes in Spain; Andersen in Denmark—all these stamps honoring famous men are expressions of cultural propaganda.

Sometimes the desire to assert cultural supremacy gives rise to two countries' claiming the same notables. When the Germans issued the Händel stamp in 1935, for example, they did so not only because it was the 250th anniversary of Händel's birth, but also, perhaps, because the British have been regarding him as an English composer. A similar motive was evidenced in stamps portraying Copernicus. The first such were put out by Poland in 1923. In 1942 and 1943, however, the German occupation authorities in Poland included Copernicus in a group of Germans shown on stamps issued for use in the area.

Economic Propaganda

Many countries have used stamps as a vehicle of economic propaganda. Since each nation is dependent on certain basic agricultural and manufactured products which it exports to further its economic stability, it is natural that these products should be given preferred attention. This is especially true of those nations which have only a few native products or industries.

The economic aspect has been mostly emphasized by Latin American countries and the overseas possessions of European powers. European countries, on the other hand, tend to publicize their industrial fairs and exhibitions.

Argentina has released a variety of stamps showing its wealth in meat, wool, sugar, oil fields and cotton. Chile has often depicted its mineral wealth, particularly nitrates and copper. Bolivia has portrayed time and again its famous tin mines. Brazil, Colombia, Venezuela, Ecuador and various Central American countries, have advertised their coffee. Cuba has shown her tobacco and sugar industries, depicting tobacco in its various stages from the growing plant in the field to the finished cigar. She has also portrayed a sugar cane plantation, an old sugar mill and a modern sugar refinery. Whether the theme is the oranges of the Pitcairn Islands, the cotton of Egypt, the rice of Indochina, the dates of French Guinea, the cod fisheries of Newfoundland, the rubber of Mozambique, the cocoa of Haiti, the guano and mineral wealth of Peru, the bananas of Jamaica, practically every nation has utilized its stamps at one time or another to advertise its products or its industries, its mines or its commerce.

Religious Propaganda

Stamps have frequently been used to convey religious propaganda in various ways.

The Vatican has long been aware of the value of stamps for the propagation of the faith. Its stamps, which are distinctly beautiful as artistic specimens, include the Papal coat of arms and the portraits of Pope Pius XI and Pope Pius XII. Later Vatican stamps have depicted such subjects as the Codex Justinianus, the proclamation of the Decretals of Gregory IX, St. John Bosco and St. Francis de Sales. During World War II, three sets of stamps bearing the figure head of Jesus Christ were issued to encourage aid to prisoners of war.

Italy printed a III Centenary of Propaganda Fide set in 1923; in 1925 and 1933 it issued stamps to commemorate those Holy Years. Portugal honored St. Antonius, her patron saint, in 1895 and 1931; in 1950 it honored the Fatima miracle. Spain has released stamps to raise funds for excavation work in the Catacombs of St. Damas and the Pretextate in Rome. It has also printed other religious stamps.

In 1933, Austria issued stamps to commemorate the defense of Christianity against the Turks. Hungary has released many stamps depicting St. Emeric, St. Stephen, and St. Elizabeth, and other great religious figures, some of whom are important as patriotic symbols.

If we look to South America, we find stamps commemorating Eucharistic Congresses or other religious events on stamps of Argentina, Bolivia, Brazil and Ecuador. Ireland, incidentally, issued a stamp in 1932 to commemorate the Eucharistic Congress of that year; in 1933 it printed a stamp in honor of the Holy Year.

8

Communist Propaganda

Political, historical, ideological, territorial, and nationalistic propaganda on stamps is now an established practice, but most nations were slow to use philately for these ends. The leader in this regard unquestionably is the Soviet Union.

Until 1917 Russian stamps were characterized by philatelic classicism—i.e., they showed only the coat of arms of the Romanov dynasty. However, the Romanov set could well be considered "dynastic propaganda", as well as historic nationalism, because it symbolizes the development and expansion of Russian might.

After 1917, the designs were at first poorly made, but once the Communists were firmly in power, they flooded the world with their stamps in the most spectacular way. Almost invariably, the regular Soviet sets, designed principally for use by persons within the Soviet Union, glorified three types of Russians—the worker, the peasant and the Red soldier.

To publicize the Soviet cause abroad, more "suitable" sets were issued; their designs included revolutionary scenes (1825, 1905, 1917, Potemkin), mass meetings of Bolshevist followers, and similar subjects calculated to have a desirable effect on minds abroad.

In recent years larger and larger stamps have been used to show the advances of the new regime. In record breaking speed Moscow issued one stamp after the other, all of which were apparently sold abroad with success.

The attempt to portray the Soviet Union in a favorable light to the rest of the world has included portraits of Russians famous in the arts (Tolstoi, Pushkin, etc.), scenes glorifying the success of the first and subsequent Five Year Plans, and pictures of Soviet buildings (some not yet erected).

Since Soviet stamps invariably appear in unused or cancelled-to-order condition, serious collectors doubt that many of them are actually used for postal purposes. To all indications, they are primarily issued for propaganda ends; it is unlikely that most of them have ever been circulated in the Soviet Union. However, they have to be recognized as legitimate stamps once the Soviet Union sends specimens to the Berne Universal Postal Union, the international organization dealing with postal matters.

Many Russian stamps have never been on sale in any Soviet post office, but are distributed or sold by a special Soviet philatelic agency in Moscow. The ultimate was reached when the Soviets even issued stamps for Tannu Tuva, a remote Siberian territory; these stamps never circulated there, but were sold in Moscow at the official philatelic agency.

As World War II approached, the Soviet Union began to issue stamps vaunting its military power—particularly its air force, infantry and navy. Later on, during the war, they showed pictures of Soviet forces in action—soldiers throwing grenades, sharpshooters, planes destroying tanks. Some of the wartime stamps also honored the workers behind the lines—miners, munition workers, etc. Some of the stamps of this period stressed the good relations existing then between the Soviet Union and the United States. At the time of the Teheran Conference (1943), a stamp released to commemorate this event bore the British, American, and Soviet flags. In the following year another stamp picturing the three flags was issued in honor of June 14, the day on which England, the United States and the Soviet Union became allies.

How far the Soviet Union has changed, however, may be seen from a stamp issued in 1949. Uncle Sam, with top hat and whiskers, is shown holding a flaming torch towards a large globe of the world. A Soviet worker extends an arm to fend off the torch. In his other hand the worker holds a banner inscribed in Russian "For Peace" and "Against the Incendiaries of War". Workers in the background carry banners "For Peace" in English and other languages.

Although Soviet stamps since 1917 have largely been instruments of Communist propaganda, they can in some instances be considered also as an appeal to nationalism. Thus the stamps honoring famous Russians, and especially the armed forces sets of World War II, are examples of this dualism.

After 1945 the satellite countries began to issue Communist propaganda. Gottwald, Stalin and Lenin appeared on Czechoslovak stamps. Hungary not only depicted Stalin and Lenin, but also put out sets commemorating Bolshevist subjects. Rumania has lately released nothing but propaganda labels in the form of stamps commemorating, for example, that country's about-face in 1944, the World Trade Union Congress of 1945, Workers' Day, and Communist youth. Bulgaria faithfully followed the same pattern with its "peace", "anti-fascist", and "partisan" issues. Poland has also used the Communist theme on its stamps, although before the Communists seized complete con-

CULTURAL PROPAGANDA

COMMUNIST PROPAGANDA

NATIONAL PROPAGANDA

COMMERCIAL PROPAGANDA

trol of the country it gave somewhat more importance to nationalistic and chauvinistic aspects. Of interest is the issue commemorating the members of the Polish Brigade in the Spanish Civil War who fought with other Leftist comrades on the Iberian peninsula.

Eastern Germany recently put out a "Youth Rally for Peace" issue and a "Friendship for China" set depicting a huge portrait of Mao Tze Tung. In regular issues for the Soviet Zone of Germany we could see a whole gallery of prominent Communists including Karl Marx, Friedrich Engels, August Bebel and Ernst Thaelmann. Logically enough, G. W. F. Hegel, father of the philosophy of the absolute mind, and Gerhard Hauptmann, the creator of German naturalism, were added for good measure.

Nationalist Propaganda

Germany, during the national-socialist government, used postage stamps in much the same manner as the Soviet Union, but with some significant differences. The craftsmanship—from a propaganda point of view—was much better and more thorough; moreover, the stamps were really used in all post offices throughout the country. German stamps of those days ranged from Frederick the Great, symbolizing the spirit of Prussia, to the new achievements of the regime, and from scenic resorts to famous men.

But nationalistic propaganda can be seen particularly in those issued in 1934 for the Saar (one year before the plebiscite), those commemorating the return of the Saar to Germany (1935), the Hitler Youth movement, and the Hitler souvenir sheets with the slogan "He Who Wants to Save a People Can Think Only in Heroic Terms". Political propaganda was also evident in the Party Rally stamps, the Hitler birthday stamps, and the January 30th memorial issues, all of which appeared annually. Other propaganda issues were those commemorating fifty years of German Helgoland, the return of Eupen and Malmedy as well as Northern Slovenia, and the symbolic union of Germany and Austria.

Cancellations were also utilized in the Third Reich. "Victory, Germany Is Winning On All Fronts" was used in Bohemia and Moravia in an attempt to impress the Czech people. In all German post offices, postcards were sold bearing slogans, phrases from Hitler speeches, etc.

Italy was keenly aware of the value of stamps as political propaganda during the Fascist era. As soon as Mussolini gained control of the country, the stamps bearing King Victor Emmanuel III were suddenly not sufficient, and an ever increasing amount of stamps, always larger and more beautiful, came forth from the Italian Engraving Bureau. Great emphasis was put upon the vigorous Roman forbears of ancient times and the illustrious Italians of the Middle Ages who had contributed so much to the culture and history of the nation. The Italian stamps of the Fascist period also portrayed the vigor of Fascism—ranging from the saluting children to the mighty Caesar-like Duce. The achievements of the regime—the reclaimed marshes, the strengthened navy, the annexation of Fiume, the conquest of Abyssinia—were all blatantly vaunted on stamps.

Most of these stamps carried their propaganda message not only through pictures, but also through slogans. In 1932 a stamp showing a statue of Mussolini bore these words: "Se avanzo, seguitemi" (If I advance, follow me!). Another stamp of the same set, showing ancient ships in the background and modern Italian ships in the foreground, bears the motto, "Il nostro destino è stato è sarà sempre sul mare" (Our destiny has been and shall always be on the sea).

During World War II, some stamps were sold with special stickers attached. The regular stamp was accompanied by a propaganda label with one of four different legends: "La vittoria sarà del Tripartito" (Victory will go to the Tripartite Powers); "Armi e cuori devono essere tesi verso la meta" (Arms and hearts must be directed towards the goal); "Tutto e tutti per la vittoria" (Everybody and everything for victory); "La disciplina è arma di vittoria" (Discipline is a weapon for victory). Postcards carried the legend across the space left for correspondence: "Vinceremmo" (We shall win).

Mussolini has gone, but nationalism on stamps has certainly continued in Italy. Propaganda has, however, turned now to the democratic ideal instead of the Roman Empire and its twentieth century Mussolini version.

Miscellaneous Political Propaganda

Both sides in the Spanish Civil War made prolific use of stamps for their partisan purposes. The Republican Government tried to show its "democratic" character by issuing a set of stamps bearing a symbol of the Republic. It overprinted many stamps emphasizing the defense of Madrid and the Republic. |To arouse sympathy in the United States, it issued its famous Statue of Liberty stamp with flags of the United States and Republican Spain in the background. |

The Nationalist forces, on the other hand, were just as active as their Republican counterparts. They made extensive use of overprints. Hundreds of special semipostal city stamps represented symbols and allegories appealing to the National Uprising, the glorious past of Spain, the need for a rebirth and a cleansing of Spanish politics. Few places in Spain lack stamps of the Civil War which were not overprinted with such legends as "Saludo a Franco" (Long live Franco) and "Arriba España" (Long live Spain). The regular stamps, issued very early during the Civil War, carried the portraits of King Ferdinand and Queen Isabella I as a symbol of Spain's union and its great past. Later, a stamp bearing the portrait of the Cid (Rodrigo Díaz de Vivar) was used as a symbol of struggle and liberation. As the Cid once liberated Valencia from the Moors, perhaps this indicated a parallel with the Leftist Government whose capital had been transferred to Valencia.

In the United States the propaganda value of stamps was duly recognized during the last war. We need only recall the three stamps promoting national defense in 1940. One showed the Statue of Liberty, another displayed an anti-aircraft battery, and the third depicted a torch as the symbol of democracy.

Besides these, there was a stamp honoring China's role in the war, several stamps bearing such legends as "Win the War" and "Freedom of Speech, and Religion, From Want and Fear", the Corregidor stamp, and the "Nations United Towards Victory" issue. But perhaps the most striking set is the so-called Flag issue, honoring the flags of thirteen countries which had been overrun by the Tripartite Powers.

In 1945 we had some other propaganda material in such stamps as the "Towards United Nations" issue, the Iwo Jima stamp, the U.S. Army stamp, and the Pulitzer Press issue. The latter stamp showed the Statue of Liberty in the background and bore the quotation "Our republic and its press will rise or fall together". The latest U.S. stamp of political propaganda is the NATO issue.

Other recent stamps of political propaganda can be seen in the Oradour (1945), Maydanek (1946), and Lidice (1947) issues commemorating massacre victims of France, Poland and Czechoslovakia; the resistance movement stamps (France, 1944; Rumania, 1945; Belgium,

1945; Yugoslavia, 1945; Luxemburg, 1946; Denmark, 1947. In 1938 Czechoslovak stamps were overprinted by Sudeten German propaganda with "Wir sind frei" (We are free) during the evacuation of the Czech authorities and the arrival of German troops; these stamps were not recognized later by the German Ministry of Posts.

Mention should also be made of the early issues of Yugoslavia (1919, for the Slovene regions), Czechoslovakia (1920), and the Kerensky issue in Russia (1917)—all of which show the symbolic breaking of chains.

The liberation of France in 1944 and of Alsace-Lorraine in 1945 was also commemorated. The "Aide aux Résistants" issue, circulated in Algiers by the French Committee of National Liberation (1943-44), and the "Tchad au Rhin" sets, released by several French colonies (1946) impressed the world with the efforts of the Free French in Africa. A few more examples are the liberation issues of Luxemburg (1945), Austria's anti-fascist set (1946), Egypt's evacuation stamp commemorating the departure of British troops from Cairo (1946), the Polish "Liga Morska" issue honoring the new Polish sea border from Stettin to Danzig, the Warsaw 1939-1945 set depicting famous buildings of that city before and after their destruction.

A striking example of political propaganda in World War II is the set of stamps issued by Cuba in 1943 to urge action against the Fifth Column menace. These stamps bore vivid pictures and exhortations.

Some countries have used stamps to carry out campaigns against illiteracy (Ecuador in 1946, Mexico in 1945). Mexico's stamp is particularly striking; it shows hands about to remove the blindfold from a man's eyes. Other countries have set forth their general political aims via philately by stressing social justice and good government.

A newcomer to the field of political propaganda is the United Nations, which in 1951 released its first stamps showing in symbolic terms the hopes of mankind for a world organization, peace and better international relations.

Distinctly pertinent is the activity of exile governments in using stamps as a propaganda weapon. During Belgium's occupation by Germans in World War I, Belgian post offices in Le Havre, France, headquarters of the Belgian government, continued to use regular Belgian stamps. Montenegro issued stamps in Bordeaux which were used for a while after the Kingdom of Serbs, Croats and Slovenes annexed Montenegro in 1918.

The occupied countries in World War II, whose governments fled to London, issued stamps for use on their ships. Poland was the first exiled government to utilize special stamps, and issued a set in December 1941 depicting destroyed monuments and the armed forces. Other sets followed later: one, commemorating the Polish struggle for liberation, appeared in 1943; another, in honor of the Polish forces fighting at Montecassino, was released in 1944.

After Germany invaded and occupied Norway, the Norwegian exile government in London overprinted regular Norwegian stamps with "V". On June 1, 1943 a special set was printed in London showing King Haakon, the Norwegian armed forces, and the legend: "Ve vil vinne" (We shall win).

Holland issued a special set on June 15, 1944, depicting Queen Wilhelmina and the Dutch armed forces in Britain; these stamps were later used in the liberated Netherlands, like the Norwegian "V" set in Norway.

Yugoslavia was another government which printed stamps in London; there was a King Peter set and an issue to commemorate the 25th anniversary of the Kingdom of Yugoslavia.

On the other hand, those countries whose governments did not flee to London during World War II also released stamps of a propagandistic nature. France's Vichy Government issued a few Pétain sets and also stamps showing the concepts of L'Etat Français—"Travail, Famille, Patrie" (Work, Family, Fatherland)—in contrast with the well-known "Liberté, Egalité, Fraternité" (1943). In Serbia there appeared a propaganda set against freemasonry, world Jewry and communism (1941).

Croatia, which considered itself liberated by the Axis, produced its first stamps in 1941, overprinting former Yugoslav King Peter II issues with the legend "Nezavisna Drzava Hrvatska" (Independent Croat State); subsequently it released a sizable number of propaganda stamps. Slovakia, which likewise felt that its independence was brought about by the Axis, issued stamps for Slovak soldiers fighting against Communism.

Mention should also be made of the various series of stamps issued in the struggle against Soviet Russia. Croatia and Rumania printed special stamps called "Comrades of Arms". The Rumanian stamps (1941) showed Rumanian and German soldiers, and the Croatian stamps (1941) Croatian, German, Italian and Hungarian soldiers. Among the stamps stressing the fight against Communism were the French "Légion Tricolore" set (1942), the Norwegian "Den Norske

Legion" set (1941, 1943), the Netherlands "Legioen" stamps (1942), and the Belgian "Légion Wallonie" and "Legioen Vlanderen" unofficial vignettes (1941-43). The latter were later not officially recognized as postage stamps, although they circulated on envelopes.

Although Croatia lost its independence in 1945, some leaders of its so-called "Exile Government" living in Argentina issued on April 10, 1951 a set of stamps commemorating the reestablishment of its state on April 10, 1941. The six stamps which appeared in Buenos Aires feature symbols with patriotic significance to every Croat—Zagreb, Split, Siroki Brijeg, Sarajevo, the Croatian Parliament, and finally a cemetery with Catholic crosses and Moslem burial stones. Inscribed in Croatian on the last mentioned stamp was: "My people is enslaved; my country is only a cemetery". This unusual set of frank propagandistic value was the subject of the following comment in the August 30, 1951, issue of *National Stamp News*, official organ of the National Philatelic Society:

"Croats in exile in South America are pressing their claim in communications received in New York last week, that six pictorial stamps printed some months ago on behalf of the 'Independent State of Croatia'—inscribed as the Nezavisna Drzava Hrvatska on the stamps—are entitled to universal recognition in standard catalogues published for the guidance of philatelists. Croatia is one of the states which form today's Yugoslavia, and the 'Independent State' represents an anti-Communist underground movement seeking Croatian independence from the Government of Marshal Tito. The regime in exile's Prime Minister is Dr. Dazfer Kulenovitch, now living in Syria according to Kent B. Styles of the New York Times.

"Writing from Buenos Aires, Prof. Janko Lukinic encloses a cover which reached the Croatian representatives in Argentina after having been mailed in Croatia. It bears three of the six pictorials. The postmark is dated June 9, 1951, and includes the name of General Boban, commander of the underground forces. The Argentine postal authorities passed the cover through the Buenos Aires post office and back-stamped it in the normal way. In lower left is pen-written 'Via Trst', indicating the cover moved by way of Trieste.

"Professor Lukinic writes that 'our government has been informed of the arrival of 372 such letters in Argentina, 27 in Uruguay, 32 in Egypt, 14 in Syria, 2 in the United States, and 44 in Italy.'

"He adds: 'The stamps were sold primarily at the counters of the post offices in Bosnia and Herzegovina—post offices which had fallen into the hands of the Croatian troops of liberation—. To name a few: Alipasin, Most, Grude, Prozor, Avtovac, Bradina.'

"Enclosed with the letter from Professor Lukinic is an eight-page document reviewing the history of the Croats' struggle for national independence. This was written by Dr. Ing. Aloisius Grandina, Undersecretary of the Office of the Prime Minister. It contains no information as to where the stamps were printed, but Dr. Grandina states that 'by means of special underground channels the stamps were sent to the Underground'. They symbolize, he writes, 'The sacred rights of a nation, enslaved by Communists, *to be heard thru philately because all other means have been stolen from it. This is the new sense and new meaning of philately in our times.'*"

Also propagandistic were the issues put out after Hitler's attack on Russia by the Provisional Government of the Ukrainian People in Lwow, those by the Ukrainian Underground after 1944 and the stamps released in Germany in 1950 by the Ukrainian National Council with the permission of the Western Allies. The latter stamps were clearly intended primarily to arouse the interest of world opinion in the fate of the Ukrainian people and to proclaim that these people still aspire to be freed one day from Communism and the Russians.

Stamps of this type are by no means new. Here are a few examples of older propaganda stamps:

(a) The so-called "Aguinaldo" set was issued by Philippine insurgents to honor their "revolutionary government" in the early days of American occupation in 1899.

(b) Carlist stamps were used in the Basque Provinces and Navarra during the insurrection of 1873-75. The second Carlist war in Spain began when the pretender Don Carlos crossed the Bidasoa River and entered the Basque Provinces, where his followers formed themselves into fighting units. Later on, as the struggle continued, postage stamps were "necessary" and stamps depicting Don Carlos with the legend "Dios, Patria, Rey" (God, Fatherland, King) were issued. Symbolizing the Traditionalist insurrection, these stamps were used to carry out propaganda in the occupied parts of Spain as well as in France, where many of Don Carlos' followers and sympathizers resided.

(c) Another example is the Hungarian overprints of 1921. The Hungarian people resented the Trianon Treaty which stipulated, among other things, the cession to Austria of a portion of land situated near the Austro-Hungarian border (Burgenland). For several

21

200693

months there appeared in that region a large number of Hungarian stamps overprinted with the following words: "Nyugatmagyarország Népe Nem Nem Soha!" (People of Western Hungary, No, No, Never!). The overprinting had been done by Hungarian patriots who briefly resisted Austrian occupation.

Propaganda stamps have also been used effectively to publicize territorial claims and counter-claims.

Sharp controversy arose in 1900 when the Dominican Republic printed stamps depicting its boundaries as including parts of Haiti.

Peru vigorously protested in 1938 when Ecuador issued a stamp showing the country's borders extending into the territory of its southern neighbor.

During the Chaco campaign, Paraguay released stamps showing the Chaco region with the legend "Chaco Paraguayo" and the words "El Chaco boreal ha sido, es y será del Paraguay" (Northern Chaco was, is and will always be Paraguayan).

In 1925 Bolivia printed a nationalistic issue (centennial commemorative set) including a stamp showing a plucked condor on the peaks of the Andes looking towards the sea, adjoining these words: "Towards the Sea". The plucked condor, the symbol of Bolivia, was gazing toward the territory which once belonged to Bolivia but is now part of Chile and Peru.

Egypt issued a stamp in 1949 showing "L'Empire d'Egypte sous le règne de Mohamed Ali, 1849-1949" (The Empire of Egypt under the reign of Mohammed Ali, 1849-1949) and depicting parts of modern Egypt, Sudan, Cyrenaica, Arabia, Palestine, Crete, Lebanon, Syria, Jordan, and Southern Turkey as belonging together.

Ireland, too, has set forth territorial claims via philately; her stamps bear a map of the entire island (including British-held Northern Ireland) by way of reiterating that the Northern portion belongs to the Irish Free State.

In 1933 Argentina refused to recognize stamps issued by the British authorities in the Falkland Islands commemorating the first centennial of British rule. Argentine recipients of letters with these stamps were requested to pay postage, just as if no stamps were attached. In 1935 Argentina issued a new set of regular stamps, including a stamp depicting Argentina's sovereignty over the Falkland Islands, and showing the frontiers of other South American republics. Britain and Peru promptly protested that the borders were not correct (Britain, because Argentina did not recognize British sovereignty over

22

the Falkland Islands; and Peru, because it considered that its border with Ecuador was not represented correctly on the stamp). A new Argentine stamp released in 1936 showed Argentina as including the Falkland Islands, but did not include the boundaries of other South American countries.

The controversy between Argentina and Great Britain became more acute when, after 1945, the race for the Antarctic lands was accelerated. Britain issued overprinted stamps for the four dependencies (South Georgia, Graham Land, South Orkneys, South Shetland) and also a set with a map of the "British" Antarctic. This aroused indignation in Argentina and Chile. Both countries promptly issued stamps for what they consider their Antarctic regions. A new Argentine stamp showing the complete territory claimed by Argentina was issued recently. Special stamps for the Antarctic have also been released in Buenos Aires and Santiago.

Symbolic Devices

As we have already seen, symbols, slogans, words, and pictures are often reflected on stamps. France uses the Republic, or Cérès, as a symbol of French liberty and democracy. German, Italian, Spanish, and Swiss stamps contain their symbols "Germania", "Italia", "Hispania", and "Helvetia". The Soviet Union uses its Communist symbols almost constantly.

The Statue of Liberty has been used on the stamps of the United States, Uruguay, Monaco, Cuba, the Spanish Republic, San Marino, Switzerland, France, Panama, Peru, Nicaragua, Brazil, Haiti. The late President Roosevelt was depicted as a symbol of democracy on stamps of Argentina, Ecuador, El Salvador, Hungary, Turkey, Indonesia, and other countries.

Friendship Stamps

Stamps honoring other countries are frequently printed by governments as a vehicle for promoting friendship or to arouse sympathy for another people. Particularly pertinent are the various issues of the United States bearing the portraits of European figures related

23

to the history of America. Such were the sets for Baron von Steuben in 1930, Pulaski in 1930, Kosciusko in 1933. Other examples are the Ericson Memorial stamp of 1926, the Pan American Union issue of 1940 and the recent Lafayette stamp. Innumerable Washington issues have appeared in many countries. Argentina, Brazil and Uruguay have often released stamps honoring their neighbors. Argentina has twice printed stamps in honor of Brazil. When a bridge was recently inaugurated on the Uruguay River by the Brazilian and Argentine presidents, a commemorative stamp issued in Argentina bore the famous words of Roque Sáenz Peña: "Todo nos une, nada nos separa" (Everything unites us, nothing separates us). Another example of this type of stamp was the U.S. issue of 1948 showing the Niagara Railway Suspension Bridge with the inscription: "A Century of Friendship—United States-Canada" honoring the friendly ties between the two countries.

In 1937 France released a stamp commemorating the U.S. Constitution, another subject which has been popular in Latin American issues.

Appreciation of the efforts of various countries (Argentina, Brazil, Chile, Peru, the United States and Uruguay) at the Buenos Aires Peace Conference to settle the Chaco war was shown by Paraguay in a 1939 issue honoring the flags and presidents of those countries, (except in the case of the United States, where the symbol of the eagle was shown instead of the President). A recent illustration of a friendship stamp is to be found in the Paraguayan 1951 Queen Isabel V Centenary issue bearing the legend "Viva España" (Long Live Spain).

Propaganda Efficacy

What is the efficacy of propaganda in philately? How efficient is propaganda in this field? There are four basic elements to consider in this connection.

(1). A stamp must have a wide circulation inside and/or outside the issuing country. This can be obtained only through adequate face value. A very low or very high value cannot serve the purpose. For example, the United States 4½ cents and $5 stamps are very rarely used and hence cannot carry a propaganda message very widely. On the other hand, the 3 cent stamp is the best guarantee for extensive

24

circulation; postal authorities usually issue commemoratives in this denomination.

(2) The designs must attract people. Stamps must be beautiful, colorful and simple: they must not be overloaded in their designs. They must have lines which attract the eye immediately and reveal its purpose instantly. The pictorial aspect is very important. Austrian, Swiss, Dutch, German, Scandinavian, and British Colonial stamps are very popular, but those of certain Latin American and Eastern European countries are not, simply because the latter do not recognize the importance of attractive design.

(3) The stamps should not be sold at excessive prices when the issues are so-called welfare stamps—i.e., stamps bearing two figures (the first covers postage, the second is intended to raise money for various welfare purposes). Thus, a stamp of 5 francs which is stamped 5 plus 45 is excessive from the stamp collector's viewpoint. This is an element which some countries apparently have heeded and which has borne fruit in the ready acceptance of welfare stamps by philatelists. Other countries, of which Belgium is one example, have lost a great many potential sales in the world markets because of an over-emphasis on costly welfare stamps.

(4) Governments should not put out too frequently expensive sets consisting of a large number of stamps. If such cases occur, the purpose is obviously a non-postal one designed to drain the pocket of the philatelist. This is detrimental to the country's philately because the stamp collector, feeling that he is imposed upon, gets an unfavorable picture of the country as a whole. Thus the propaganda effect is substantially diminished.

That propaganda in stamps is effective is seen in the fact that Germany prohibited the sale of Soviet stamps from 1933 to 1939, and from 1941 to 1945. The United States did not allow the sale of German stamps after 1941 and based this on the "Trading with the Enemy Act". The Western Allies recently revoked an ordinance which forbade dealings in occupied Germany in any German stamps bearing the portrait of Hitler. Currently the sale of North Korean and Red Chinese stamps is forbidden in the United States, principally to prevent the Communists from accumulating dollars.

Propaganda on Cancellations

Like stamps, the cancellation is also used for a wide variety of propaganda purposes. Most countries employ it to advertise governmental campaigns or measures for comparatively brief periods. In some cases the cancellation takes the form of friendly advice. Certain nations like the United States, Argentina, England, Belgium, Switzerland, Germany have made extensive use of cancellations.

Taking the United States as a first example, there have been many different subjects appearing as cancellation items. There is the well known cancellation "Air Mail Saves Time", or the one which was used in New York at the peak of its terrible water shortage: "Save Water". In 1950 at eleven different post offices throughout the country the United States used a slogan cancellation boosting aid to Europe and reading "Marshall Plan, Partnership for Peace". More recent cancellations have urged support for the Red Cross, the March of Dimes, the Heart Fund, and other worthy causes.

Argentina and Chile are using cancellations on envelopes mailed in their Antarctic possessions which "show the flag", demonstrating the de facto occupation of various points. The four Argentine bases (San Martin, South Orkneys, Deception Island and Melchior Island) use the cancellation "Antártida Argentina" and name of the base. The Chilean bases (Port Sovereignty, González Videla and O'Higgins) utilize the cancellation "Territorio Chileno Antártico" (Chilean Antarctic Territory).

When President Vargas came to Buenos Aires in 1935, the following cancellation was put on the envelopes: "Los pueblos argentino y brasileño están unidos por convenios de paz y trabajo" (The Argentine and Brazilian peoples are united by agreements of peace and work). Few countries have sponsored so much propaganda on cancellations as Argentina. Its postal authorities have, for example, urged the public through cancellations to ventilate their bedrooms thoroughly, to eradicate locusts, to contribute funds for the blind, to celebrate Pan-American Day, and even to see the doctor before marrying.

On Belgian and German envelopes the cancellation has been used for another purpose—to encourage the destruction of the potato bug. In Belgium little stickers with the legend "Le doryphore ménace vos récoltes, détruisez-le!" (The potato bug endangers your harvest, destroy it!) were posted on envelopes beside a picture showing the deadly enemy of European agriculture. Apparently the usual means to destroy this terrible pest were not enough, so the authorities decided to call on the postal services as well.

An interesting and humorous Danish cancellation draws attention to the fact that radio listeners are tuning in too loud and are kindly requested to turn down the radio. A cartoon of a man in pajamas and with hands to his ears, has with it the words: "Daemp Radioen" (tune down the radio).

An appeal to patriotism in historic terms, an almost universal trend, is shown in Switzerland, where in 1948 three different cancellations were used to commemorate events related to Swiss history: 100 years of the Federal State, the Neuchâtel Revolution, the Peace of Westphalia.

How effective is the cancellation? It appeals to people through the use of words and slogans which are comprehensive and simple—so that they can be read at a glance. As envelopes and postcards have an enormous circulation, the cancellation helps greatly to carry out official campaigns. In short, the cancellation, appealing with headlines and slogans, is the ideal complement to the stamp which is a propaganda instrument based more on pictures, symbols, colors and the like, and not so much on words. The cancellation can say in slogans what the stamp expresses at the same time with a symbol, an allegory, in an artistic manner full of attractive colors and pictures. Both together are immensely valuable for any propaganda aim.

Conclusion

The postage stamp and the cancellation are both very effective means of propaganda, as they influence large segments of the population, and reach an even wider public than television, radio or movies. Although widely exploited as a propaganda medium only in the last twenty years, the postage stamp and the cancellation are now everywhere used to serve propaganda purposes, and are used for touristic, cultural, economic, religious, political, and ideological ends. The future will certainly witness an even greater application of propaganda techniques to philately.

CPSIA information can be obtained
at www.ICGtesting.com
Printed in the USA
BVHW09005118012 2
626439BV00010B/442